Directions In Art

Photography

Debbie Humphry

www.heinemann.co.uk/library
Visit our website to find out more information about Heinemann Library books.

To order:
- Phone 44 (0) 1865 888066
- Send a fax to 44 (0) 1865 314091
- Visit the Heinemann Bookshop at www.heinemann.co.uk/library to browse our catalogue and order online.

First published in Great Britain by Heinemann Library, Halley Court, Jordan Hill, Oxford OX2 8EJ, part of Harcourt Education.
Heinemann is a registered trademark of Harcourt Education Ltd.

Editorial: Lucy Thunder and Helen Cannons
Design: Jo Hinton-Malivoire and AMR
Picture Research: Hannah Taylor and Elaine Willis
Production: Edward Moore

Originated by Ambassador Litho Ltd
Printed and bound in China by South China Printing Company

ISBN 0 431 17647 7
07 06 05 04 03
10 9 8 7 6 5 4 3 2 1

British Library Cataloguing in Publication Data
Humphry, Debbie
Photography. – (Directions in art)
770
A full catalogue record for this book is available from the British Library.

Acknowledgements
The Publishers would like to thank the following for permission to reproduce photographs: British Museum p**47**; Henri Cartier-Bresson / Magnum Photos p**5**; Eggleston Artistic Trust, Courtesy of A & C Anthology p**7;** Paul Graham / Anthony Reynolds Gallery p**6**; Joy Gregory pp**9**, **10**; Andreas Gursky / DACS, London 2003, Courtesy of Gallery Monika Sprueth Cologne pp**12**, **14**; David Hockney pp**16**, **17**, **19**; Nick Knight pp**21**, **22**, **23**; Annie Leibovitz pp**24**, **25**, **26**; Duane Michals, Courtesy of Pace / MacGill Gallery, New York pp**29**, **30 top**, **30 bottom**; Martin Parr / Magnum Photos pp**33**, **35**; Sebastio Salgado / nbpictures.com p**37**, **38**; Cindy Sherman pp**40**, **41**; Jeff Wall p**46**; Gillian Wearing p**49**.

Cover photograph of *Shoe Fashion* (1997) by Martin Parr is reproduced with permission of Martin Parr / Magnum Photos.

The Publishers would like to thank Richard Stemp, Gallery Educator at the Tate, London, for his assistance in the preparation of this book.

CONTENTS

Any words appearing in the text in bold, **like this**, are explained in the Glossary.

From its beginnings, photography, with its use of a machine instead of a person's hand to create an image, challenged the definition of art.

The camera was invented long before the pictures it made could be captured and kept as prints. Early cameras caught light reflecting from a scene by passing it through a pinhole, and later a lens, into a light-tight box, so that the scene appeared on a flat surface at the back. In the 16th century artists used cameras as drawing tools, tracing the images they formed as a basis for their pictures. By the beginning of the 19th century, scientists, painters and scholars in England and France were racing to find light-sensitive materials that could capture and keep the images made by cameras. In France, Nicephore Niepce and L.J.M. Daguerre found a way to record and **fix** the camera images on to metal plates in 1827. However, the first person to make and fix images permanently on to paper was Englishman William Henry Fox Talbot, in 1839. He used light sensitive silver chemicals and the **negative-positive** system that is the basis of what today we call photography.

A smaller camera

Photography, especially **reportage**, blossomed after World War I. In the 1920s, the **35 mm camera** was invented. This was a small format camera, taking 35 mm film. It was smaller and more portable than any previous cameras. Professional photographers no longer needed a tripod or artificial lighting, and could take photographs in all kinds of situations, indoors and outdoors, without being noticed. Politicians and famous people were captured off-guard and ordinary people were photographed on a grand scale.

Documentary photography

Alongside the launch of *Life* magazine in the USA (1936) and *Picture Post* magazine in Britain (1938) there was an explosion of photographic images in the media (then newspapers and magazines and now the TV and Internet). Both magazines ran countless picture stories exploring every aspect of human life. For the first time people could see images from foreign places, the everyday lives of working class people or behind the scenes of government.

This style of **candid** black and white photography was dominant for 50 years and is called '**documentary**'. It is still hugely influential. In 1947 a group of documentary photographers, including Frenchman Henri Cartier-Bresson (b 1908), founded their own photographic agency, Magnum, in Paris. The agency, set up for **photojournalists**, became known for its excellence and still has that reputation today.

Henri Cartier-Bresson

Born in France in 1908, Henri Cartier-Bresson is known best for his candid pictures of everyday life. 'The Decisive Moment' was a phrase he used to describe the instant of picture-taking when **composition**, meaning and feeling all came together. He used a 35mm Leica camera with a **standard lens** to give the same view as the human eye sees. He worked in black and white and carried a minimum of equipment. He also liked to work without being noticed and never **cropped** a photograph. Worldwide many photographers took up his philosophy and style of working.

Lock at Bongival France *(1955) by Cartier-Bresson is an example of a moment in time captured on camera with the viewer looking on.*

Early documentarists

Campaigning photographers, such as the American Lewis Hine (1874–1940) in the first decades of the 20th century and Dorothea Lange (1895–1965) in the 1930s, always showed the dignity of their subjects. They hoped to bring about social change by highlighting the hardships many people endured. Documentary images often celebrated life and this was well represented in *The Family of Man* exhibition in New York in 1955, which gathered together photographs of family life from all over the world. However, in the 1950s television became widespread and took over photography's role of showing us the world.

Colour photography

The first colour photographs (autochromes) were marketed by the Lumiére brothers in France in 1904. As the century progressed, colour was used by amateurs and professionals for snapshots, commercial fashion and advertising shots. It was rarely used for art photography. In the 1960s it began to be used by serious photographers such as Americans Helen Levitt (b. 1918) and William Eggleston (see page 7). Even in the 1970s, when British Paul Graham (b. 1956) photographed English social security offices in colour, people were shocked. They thought the use of colour made serious issues seem trivial.

Baby, DHSS Office, Birmingham, 1984 *by Paul Graham (1985). The pink colour of the girl's dress was considered too happy for the subject matter.*

William Eggleston

William Eggleston was born in Memphis, Tennessee, USA in 1939. His exhibition at The Museum of Modern Art, in New York, in 1976 was shocking because it consisted entirely of colour photographs. Initially people did not understand why he wanted to photograph everyday objects – the remnants of a finished meal, some earth or a crumpled newspaper. Now Eggleston is recognized as a pioneer for his use of colour and his observation of mundane, everyday details.

Greenwood Mississippi *(1973), by Eggleston focuses attention on an ordinary light bulb. He captures a surprising beauty with vivid colour and unusual angles.*

Photography today

Up until fairly recently, photography was kept separate from the mainstream art world. However, around the beginning of the 1990s it began to be shown in art galleries alongside art such as painting and sculpture. Photography now contributes to debates about truth, our culture and the role of the image.

In the last decade, photographers have challenged accepted viewpoints in a variety of ways. They encourage us to question our world and also the presumed truth of what we see in a photograph – exposing its tricks and illusions. Even today, when we know digital technology can alter a photograph, we still tend to believe what we see. Photographers began to use many different techniques beyond the strictly photographic to communicate their ideas, such as text, paint and computer technology. The photographers covered in this book represent the wide and exciting range of working methods and ideas used by photographers today.

JOY GREGORY

Joy Gregory uses photographic processes to explore themes such as memory, female beauty and history. Born in Bicester in the UK in 1959, Gregory trained at The Royal College of Art, London. She has exhibited worldwide, received numerous awards and lectures in photography. As a black British woman of Jamaican origins, Gregory is interested in exploring issues of **identity**.

> *History is the story we tell ourselves to define and outline an identity. These stories need not be totally true, but must be believable. They tell us who we are, what we are and how we are.*
> JOY GREGORY

Working methods

Gregory uses a variety of methods to communicate her ideas. She photographs in black and white and colour and has experimented with double **exposures**, toning, the Internet and installation. An installation is a way of displaying art where the way the work fits into its surroundings is part of the art. Gregory has studied **photochemistry** and produced images without the use of a camera by reworking 19th century printing techniques. She continually explores technique, but always to add to the ideas in her work. Using an old technique, for example, can result in a faded, romantic feel, giving a sense of nostalgia to the subject matter.

Exploring Caribbean culture

Gregory explored the themes of history and identity with projects such as *Memory and Skin* (1998), exhibited as an installation. She travelled to the Caribbean and, by collecting stories across the generations, pieced together the character of Caribbean culture. For the exhibition Gregory used photographs, text, video, sound and collected objects – such as postcards, a machete and a bottle of rum. These were displayed in museum glass cases to remind us how history is selected, stolen and contained out of context – how it is a story, just one version of the truth. The installation's fragmented elements suggest the complex mix created by the different origins of Caribbean people. Along with the original population there are people who have come from Africa, Asia and the Middle East. Gregory uncovers how the Caribbean's history of colonialism (dominance of one country over another) and slavery created a rich mix of religion, skin colour and language, but how it also split up a sense of identity.

Shop Window *from the project* Memory and Skin *explores the themes of history and identity by showing a black doll and the reflection of a real person in the shop window.*

Using technology

In 1998 Gregory created *The Blondes*, which was designed as an interactive website. It explores the way different types of identity influence each other across the world by looking at what it means to be blonde, particularly a 'Black Blonde'. She mixes interviews with text, photographs and **graphics**. Gregory uses the Internet to show this work because its rapid international communication echoes the way ideas and desires, such as the desire to be blonde, are spread globally. This is a good example of how Gregory uses technique to communicate her ideas.

Elegance

Gregory had the idea for a series of images of handbags, of which *Elegance* is one, while in Johannesburg, South Africa in 1997–98. Luxury goods, bought by the upper classes, fascinate her. Through these images, Gregory focuses our attention on the deeper meaning of everyday objects such as gloves and handbags. The system of apartheid, which separated white people and black people by law, allowing black people no political power, was abolished in South Africa in 1989. For the first time, a black party was allowed to stand for government and black people gained equal access to jobs and places. However, what Gregory saw in South Africa nearly 10 years later told a different story. Mostly it was the white people who had the money and positions of power and the black people still faced prejudice daily.

Gregory's handbags, with their exterior glamour and hidden interiors, seemed to symbolize South African society, where politics are not as they appear. The black and white divide is not straightforward. Some of the rich white women were the most vigorous protestors against apartheid, their class and racial power allowing them to take to the streets when the black women would not have dared. Yet Gregory found that the rich South African women who owned the handbags often seemed powerless within their own white culture, which still clung to traditional female roles. By using the handbags as symbols, Gregory shows us the inequalities and contradictions she found in South Africa.

> *Handbags are the ultimate symbol of female privacy and power. For many women this is their only private space.* JOY GREGORY

Salt print technique

Gregory collected handbags while in South Africa and used them back in England to make salt print images. She made her own light-sensitive photographic paper using a heavy cotton paper suitable for lengthy soaking in liquid chemicals. Treating about ten sheets at a time, she brushed a salting solution on to one side of the paper. This was done in daylight. Once dry, she sensitized the paper to light by brushing on a solution of silver nitrate, which is a silver chemical that reacts to light. This was done in indoor **tungsten light** because the silver nitrate is sensitive to daylight. The sheets dried in a darkened room. To make the images she placed a handbag on to a sheet of paper in daylight. The light made the paper go brown, leaving a white handbag shape where it blocked the light. She exposed the prints for 3 to 20 minutes, depending on the brightness of the light (less light needs a longer time). In areas, the brushstrokes of the chemical coatings created a textured effect. When the colour was dark enough, Gregory washed off the silver nitrate in a tray of running water, which de-sensitized the paper to stop it going any darker. Then she **fixed** the prints in sodium thiosulphate followed by a final wash. This is the original process that Fox Talbot invented (see page 4).

Photograms

The handbag salt prints are **photograms**, not traditional photographs, because they are not taken with a camera. They record only a trace of the original objects. The soft, layered texture of the prints gives a nostalgic feel to Gregory's images and reflects her interest in the past. The placing of the objects on their own within the frame takes them out of context. They become icons – objects to be admired and worshipped, but not held or owned.

ANDREAS GURSKY

Andreas Gursky makes huge colour photographs, some over 3 metres across. He has photographed places all over the world, including ski slopes, factory interiors, raves, the international stock exchange and hotels.

Gursky was born in Germany in 1955. He trained at the Düsseldorf School in Germany in the late 1970s which was run by photographers Hilla and Bernd Becher. Their ordered **compositions** and careful use of light was an influence on Gursky. Gursky graduated as a Master Pupil in 1987, has exhibited widely and has been very influential himself.

Approach

As with traditional **documentary** photography, the settings of Gursky's pictures are real and he generally changes nothing of the original scene when taking shots. But he chooses the place from which he takes the picture carefully, so that his compositions have a strong **graphic** quality, where shapes and lines are perfected into a careful order. The pictures are light and brightly coloured.

Union Rave *(1995). Gursky's photographs explore the relationship between the public and the personal, often shooting large numbers of people together.*

Gursky controls the shapes and lines in the photographs by use of technology, so that the picture we see represents the way he sees the world, rather than exactly how the world looks: he is showing us his idea about reality. His father and grandfather were also photographers and the young Gursky's bedroom was an extension of his parents' advertising studio and was used as a set (like a film set).

His most personal space would be arranged to create a make-believe place, which would then become a glossy image in a magazine. So from a young age Gursky saw the links between the real world, the created set and its visual representation.

Research

Gursky spends a huge amount of time, sometimes years, researching his subject matter. He visits locations, reads about his subject matter and studies other art to work out the best way to show visually what he is interested in and wants to communicate. A photograph may be taken in a split second, but the thinking, planning and development of ideas leading up to this moment takes much longer.

Public aims

Gursky was part of the movement in the 1980s and 1990s that gave photography the same status as other art forms and saw it displayed in mainstream galleries. The full impact of Gursky's large images is best appreciated in a gallery space. The viewer can enjoy the overall design from a distance or walk in close and be drawn into the detail. Their combination of organized structure and clarity of light and colour is visually awe-inspiring.

Influences

Gursky's photographs deliberately remind the viewer of other types of images. They refer, for example, to traditional landscape painting, **Abstract Expressionist** paintings, advertising photography and film. This mix of influences can trigger the memory and bring different styles and ideas from different times in history to mind. It is as if there is a whole set of unseen images just below the surface.

99 Cent

99 Cent (1999, 207cm x 337 cm), taken in an American cost-cutting supermarket, is recognizable to any Western shopper. The repetition of the '99 Cent' and '3.99' signs exaggerate the sense of sameness and order, so Gursky is showing the rigid structure within which we live and behave. The repetition of the parallel horizontal lines suggests that the view continues endlessly beyond the frame. It also means there is no central focus to the picture and our eyes wander along the aisles giving a sense of motion to the still quality of the picture. This is typical of Gursky's photographs. The shoppers are dwarfed by the structure of the superstore, fitting within the overall design, so that we do not see them as individuals.

The sameness of the goods reminds us that in modern life the world is structured into packages and images for us to consume. With a pair of designer jeans, for example, it is not the good quality denim of the jeans themselves that attracts us, but the glamour attached to the name. We are purchasing the look, the package, which then transfers to the wearer. Gursky is reminding us that we associate ideas with what we see. This theme of packaging and containing the world is repeated in all Gursky's pictures. He does this by his structured framing of the image and his subject matter – such as flats, factories, hotels and Prada shoe displays.

Technique

Gursky uses a **large format camera**, which takes large sheet film. At this size, it is possible to capture a huge amount of fine detail which is visible when the images are enlarged to the massive print size that Gursky exhibits.

The effect of the detail and the saturated (rich, deep) colours of the c-types is to give a 'super-real' feel to the images. This emphasizes the feeling that we are looking at an idea about a scene rather than the scene itself.

Computer technology

Since 1992 Gursky has used **post-digital manipulation**. After taking pictures he exaggerates the abstract shapes by straightening horizons, repeating lines, enhancing the colour and deleting details. When seeing the final result we do not know what he has done and there remains a sense that he is showing us the scene exactly as it was in life. He produces images that would not be possible with conventional photography.

In *99 Cent* Gursky has altered the image so that the foreground (front of the picture) and background appear to be a similar distance away: the light and colour is kept the same throughout the picture, so there is no sense of darkening or shadows in the background. The natural sense of depth and perspective is therefore lost. This flattens the image and emphasizes the lines.

Gursky sees the world as a place that has been structured and ordered by the humans that function within it. So he sees his digital intervention not as a way to change reality, but as a way to show the reality as he sees it.

DAVID HOCKNEY

David Hockney is a respected artist who is endlessly curious and experimental. Born in Yorkshire, UK, in 1937, he has been based in Los Angeles since 1964. Although Hockney has taken photographs since the 1960s, he didn't come to photography as a serious **medium** until the 1980s. It is hard to place Hockney in a category; as well as painting and photography, he has used a range of printing techniques in his work: the fax, photocopiers, cut-out images and **typography**. His work is generally figurative (representing figures or objects) and he is often linked with early British **Pop Art**. Hockney's work is easy to look at because the images are often realistic and brightly coloured. He uses snapshot-style photographs and uses everyday life for his subject matter. He is interested in communicating a message and being easily understood.

A new approach

Hockney experimented obsessively with the camera for 4 to 5 years (between 1982 and 1986), making **photo-collages**. He rejected the use of a single photograph, however carefully constructed or beautiful. Instead he took numerous images of details of a scene, and joined the many photographs together to make one picture. He called these pictures 'joiners'. Hockney believed that using only one photograph was theatrical and unnatural and could not represent reality. His multiple images showed different aspects of a scene and therefore were a better way of re-creating real vision: the eye can jump from one thing to the next, picking up clues and taking in details randomly. Some of his images have a 180-degree view, recreating the turn of our heads.

Yellow Guitar Still Life, Los Angeles, 3rd April 1982, *is a reference to the Cubist artists, Picasso and Braque. The guitar is a Cubist* ***motif*** *(often used by Cubist artists in paintings).*

> *Photography is all right if you don't mind looking at the world from the point of view of a cyclops – for a split second. But that's not what it's like to live in the world, or to convey the experience of living in the world.* DAVID HOCKNEY

Hockney started by using instant Polaroids, then progressed to one-hour **processed** photographs using **colour negative** film. This snapshot film gave a very different effect to the beautifully printed black and white images of the traditional photographer. His technique and his use of multiple images were met as a challenge to existing photographic practice. His subject matter was seen as flimsy because in practice Hockney photographed his own life. Hockney's rejection of the single image, his use of colour snapshots and interest in the everyday and the autobiographical is now recognized as pioneering and influential.

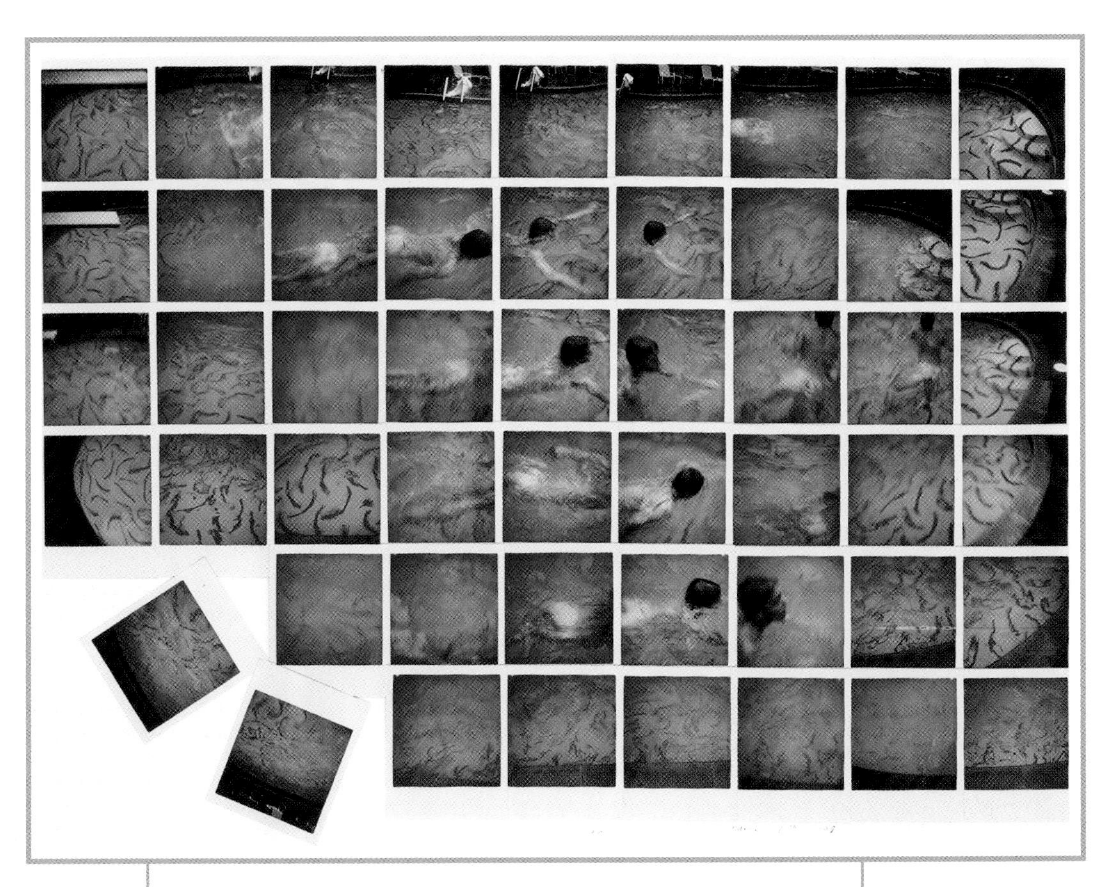

Ian Swimming, Los Angeles, March 11th 1982, *is one of Hockney's earlier 'joiners' made up of polaroid shots.*

Building pictures

The Polaroids that Hockney used for the first few months had a square **format**, vivid colours and white borders. Arranged in horizontal and vertical rows, they formed a grid. Hockney needed to achieve a convincing overall picture using the Polaroid camera's **fixed wide-angle lens**. He chose a position from which the scene would be viewed, then built up the image using a series of close-ups. He then laid the images out on the floor and built up a picture – a process that could take hours.

Space and distance

Hockney has worked for the opera and ballet, creating stage sets and backdrops in which he had to relate the figures to their backgrounds. This experience was valuable in his joiners when he had to calculate at what distance and perspective his photographs would work together with a convincing sense of space.

Sunday Morning, Mayflower Hotel, New York, 28 November 1982

Sunday Morning... (1982) is a good example of the later joiners Hockney made. After several months he stopped using the Polaroid camera and began using a Pentax. The new camera changed the joiners in several ways. Its format was rectangular which allowed much more flexibility in arranging the photographs together – they no longer had to be laid out in a grid. *Sunday Morning...* shows how the absence of a white border allows the photographs to be joined in a more natural, less formal way. The Pentax had three lenses, including a **telephoto lens**. This meant that Hockney could take close-ups without having to physically move close. All the photographs for *Sunday Morning...* could be taken from the bed. In other images the different lenses meant that Hockney could capture scenes through a car window, on a plane, an underground train or on the street. The Pentax's electronic shutter was almost silent so Hockney could more easily take photographs unobserved. The different lenses give a better match to the human eye than the Polaroid's wide-angle. Different photographs in *Sunday Morning...* were taken with different **exposures**, recording the scene lighter or darker. This gives a sense of the light changing over time. So instead of the picture being a frozen moment in time, it shows the passing of time.

Working method

Developing the pictures later with one-hour processing, rather than waiting the two to three minutes per Polaroid, speeded up the taking process. Also because

they were developed after the event and not on-the-spot, Hockney had to work out in advance how to join the separate photographs and what distances, lenses and framings he needed for the final image to look right. He had to hold the whole picture in his head instead of building it up as he went along which forced him to plan and think about the images carefully.

Autobiography

In *Sunday Morning...* we can see Hockney in the mirror, camera in hand, and we see a hand on the bedspread in the foreground. This could be his own hand or it could be someone else's. We are left to figure this out for ourselves. We see his ashtray, pair of glasses, a discarded shoe and the papers he is reading. Hockney believes that all photographs are autobiographical because the photographer has to be there to take the picture. Because Hockney wants his images to be truthful, he leaves traces of his presence in them.

Influences

Hockney's use of colour and his documentation of everything ordinary have linked him with photographer William Eggleston and the cinematic style of American painter Edward Hopper (1882–1967). Hopper captured the loneliness of life through everday subject matter. Hockney's fragmented joiners have similarities with the various angles used by Cubist painters – Cubism is an art movement in which the world is shown from a fragmented and broken-up perspective.

NICK KNIGHT

Nick Knight is one of the most sought after and influential fashion photographers today. He was born in London in 1958 and graduated from Bournemouth and Poole College of Art & Design in 1982. Knight has worked on top magazine titles, such as *Arena, Vogue* and *Wallpaper*, for fashion catalogues, advertising campaigns, exhibitions and books. He has won many awards.

Knight constantly experiments, using an imaginative set of technical tools and visual ideas. His images are stylish and posed. They have a strong sense of design, with dramatic colour, shape, line and pattern. He always gives a new view of the familiar and challenges the conventional fashion images. His work is continually developing because he is constantly excited by the **medium**.

> *I always want to go to the studio thinking how brilliant and how exciting it is to take pictures. I want to learn. I want to discover.*
> NICK KNIGHT

Post-punk

Knight's career took off in the mid-1980s following the explosion of punk in the late 1970s. Fashion, music, photography and magazine design were being transformed. Initially photography was used by designers along with other visual tools to create a mixed look: photographs were cut up, photocopied and tilted and existing photographs were re-used, often in shocking new ways. In the early 1980s, *i-D* and *The Face* magazines were launched with their more sophisticated version of the punk cut-and-mix look. Post-punk fashion took traditional styles and then changed or mixed them in unusual ways. So a smart suit might be worn with massive platform shoes. This challenge to conservative fashion was soon followed by a new direction in photography that questioned and rejected established styles. Knight worked with *i-D*'s editor and art director, Terry Jones, and was at the forefront of the new experimentation with fashion photography.

Challenging stereotypes

Knight challenges the idea of what is beautiful by choosing models who do not fit the usual fashion **stereotype**. He rejects the idea that an attractive woman has to be young and thin, by using older or plumper models. He took photographs of curvy model Sophie Dahl that appeared in *i-D* magazine, altering them on computer to make her look even plumper. In 1996 he used 80-year-old ranchers for a Levi jeans' campaign.

Aimee Mullins' Running Legs

Aimee Mullins' Running Legs is the front cover shot from a series for *Dazed and Confused* magazine in 1998, in which Knight, in collaboration with fashion designer Alexander McQueen, produced photographs using models with disabilities. His images questioned what we accept as beautiful and changed the way we look at disability. Aimee Mullins, an amputee, is photographed with the artificial legs she uses for running. The first impact of the image is the strong lines and elegant shape – then we notice the legs. The effect of beauty and agility coupled with disability is surprising but not shocking. The disability is not hidden – instead we are shown its grace and power. Knight presents us with our own prejudices, by forcing us to see things in a different way. Disabled models had never been used in fashion photography before and there were various positive effects. The images prompted a debate in the media and one of the models appeared in a television advert and play. The photographs have been shown in the Tate and are studied on various college and university courses.

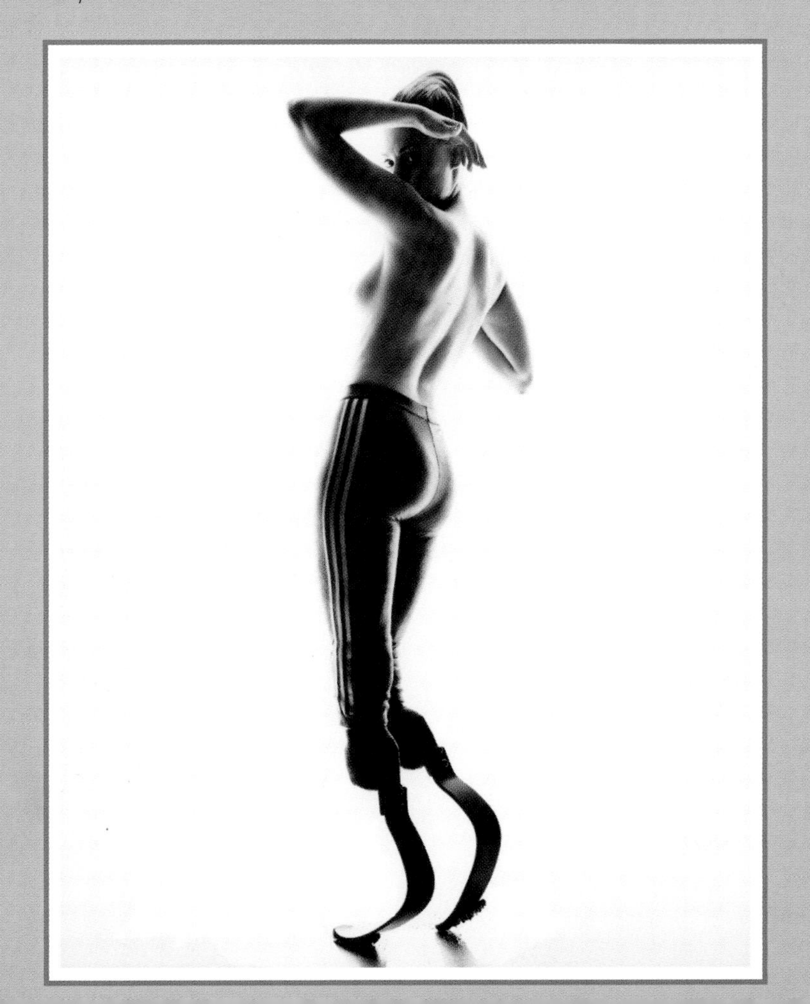

Tools and techniques

A technological explorer, Knight paints and inks on negatives and has experimented with X-ray photography and the **electron microscope**. He uses **post-digital manipulation**, changing his photographs on the computer. Knight is very excited by web sites and the Internet, which he considers a freer and more personal way of communicating than television. Knight refers to himself as an image-maker rather than a photographer. He usually uses a **large format camera**. Its size, and the time it takes to compose each shot, ensures that the subject is aware of what is going on.

Development

In the late 1980s, Knight worked with the fashion designer Yohji Yamamoto on his high quality, glossy fashion catalogues. 'Surprise me', said Yamamoto, 're-show me my dreams'. The large **format** of the fashion catalogue inspired Knight. He photographed his models and the clothes as simple forms within the white space of the page. This control of the images made the models into **abstract** surfaces of colour and movement. Rather than just showing us a simple reproduction, the images conveyed the idea of the clothes.

Naomi Campbell, taken for Yohji Yamamoto in Paris, 1987. Knight used special techniques to dramatically colour and flatten the shapes.

Fashion photography

Knight is working during a time when Western culture is obsessed with fashion and style. The significance of fashion imagery has altered since the 1960s, becoming increasingly seductive and sophisticated. Fashion photographs now do more than just sell clothes. By showing images of ideal beauty and lifestyles, they are a guide: telling us what to wear, what to do, who with and where. These images feed our obsessions and insecurities; they influence our sense of **identity**, our tastes, attitudes and sexuality. So Knight's challenge to conventional ideas about age, disability and gender are of great significance.

Branching out

Knight says his interest is not in fashion but in experimentation and beauty. He worked with botanists from The London Natural History Museum, for example, to produce striking images of dried flowers for a book, *Flora*, in 1995. It took Knight three years to select and photograph the flowers. He makes us see the flowers with a new eye, as they remind us variously of paper, string, architectural drawings, neon feathers and childrens' drawings.

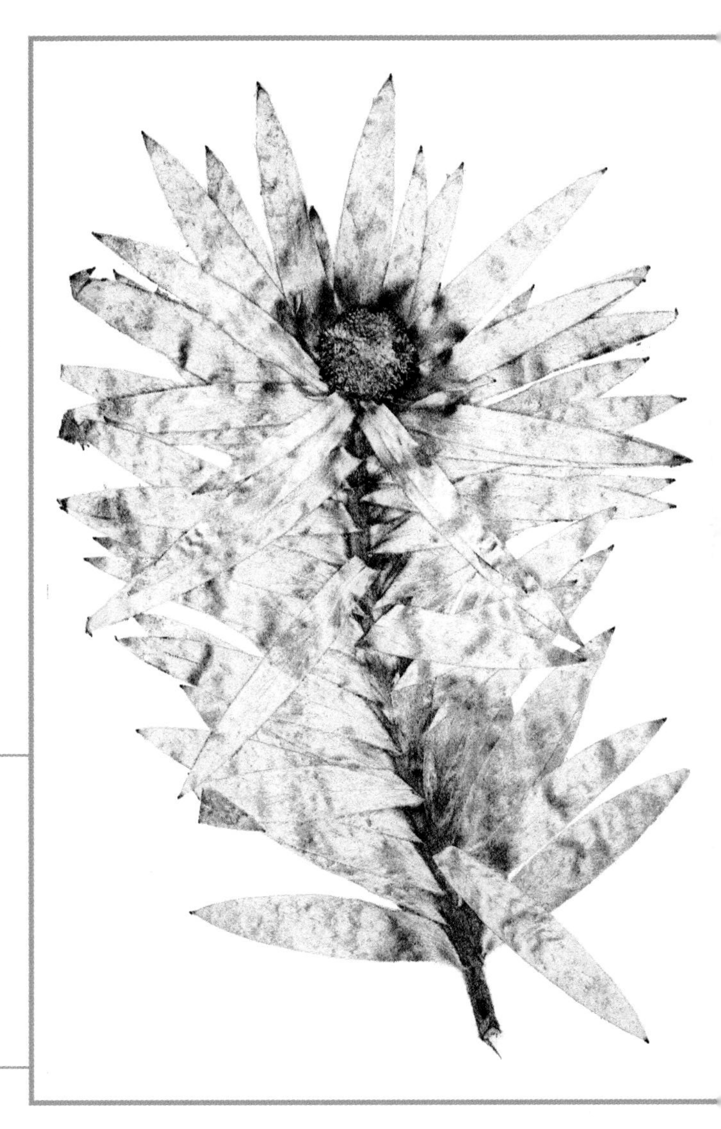

Image 10 *from* Flora *(1995) is an example of Knight's photographs of dried flowers. The images capture the plants' charm and fragility.*

ANNIE LEIBOVITZ

New Yorker Annie Leibovitz is renowned for her bold, inventive photographs of celebrities. Her subjects include musicians, politicians, athletes, artists and dancers and she works for commercial clients, such as magazines and advertising agencies. Leibovitz was born in Connecticut in 1949. She worked for the fashionable music magazine, *Rolling Stone* in the 1970s. When the stylish *Vanity Fair* magazine was re-launched in the early 1980s, Leibovitz's stunning front covers were associated with its massive success. She has exhibited all over the world.

> *I can never forget the sensation of being at a news-stand and seeing for the first time my photograph transformed into the Rolling Stone cover. It was a lot different to having a photograph floating around in the wash, or pinned on a bulletin board at school.*
> ANNIE LEIBOVITZ

The Rolling Stones on the Road, *(1975) is an example of Leibovitz's early black and white* ***documentary*** *work. She spent a lot of time with the Rolling Stones on tour.*

Photographing people

To achieve the **candid**, fly-on-the-wall style of photography for *Rolling Stone* magazine, Leibovitz involved herself in the pop-stars' lives. She stayed up all hours on tour to get informal, behind-the-scenes pictures. With the more formal style of shot for *Vanity Fair* magazine, Leibovitz often visits the sitter's house or even lives with them for a few days. Although many people are involved with making these highly controlled shots – agents, publicists, stylists and assistants – Leibovitz manages to create and sustain an intimacy with her subjects.

Style

Leibovitz started by taking black and white photographs for *Rolling Stone* magazine. In the 1980s, she developed a new style while working for *Vanity Fair*, producing high quality colour portraits. With humour and a sense of design, some aspect of her sitter was echoed in the set-up of the photograph. For the famous shot of musician John Lennon and his wife Yoko Ono in 1980, Leibovitz exposed Lennon's vulnerability by photographing him curled up naked against the clothed Ono. Her pictures are revealing, imaginative and thoughtful.

Images of our time

Leibovitz' takes her celebrity photographs at a time of growing public obsession with glamorous images of the rich and famous. Her pictures present the subjects as icons to be worshipped rather than ordinary humans. They represent the age in which she lives. Their humour includes the viewer in the careful construction of the image of a famous person. We can laugh at the leaf-coat worn by singer David Byrne or mud-covered actress/model Lauren Hutton, but we are laughing with the subject who is aware of the extreme pose they are taking. The subjects are turned almost into sculptures and become symbols of themselves. They are in on the joke too, always confident that Leibovitz will retain their glamour and style.

American Soldiers and the Queen of the Negritos *(1968). Leibovitz often uses family as a theme in her work. She said of this photograph: 'There's a photograph of my mother's family that's very similar to this one.'*

Influences

Leibovitz says one of her biggest influences are family pictures. She looks at the way the pictures are taken and what they communicate. 'You see us happy, or in thin times, whatever, for better or worse. The history of the family is there in those photographs.'

Leibovitz is part of a tradition of studio portrait photographers, including the early French studio photographer Félix Nadar (1820–1910), the English celebrity portraitist Cecil Beaton (1904–80) and the journalistic portraitist, American Diane Arbus (1923–71).

Whoopi Goldberg, Berkeley, California, 1984

Typical of Leibovitz, this photograph of actress Whoopi Goldberg (1984) is funny and surprising, with a strong **graphic composition**. The image holds clues, contradictions and questions beneath the perfect surface. Bathing in milk reminds the viewer of Cleopatra, a beautiful queen in Ancient Egypt, and her luxurious femininity. Yet what could have been a slightly shocking semi-nude shot is actually childlike.

Rolling on her back with her tongue sticking out, Goldberg looks like a puppy waiting for a tickle. Her expression is funny and links to Goldberg's work as a comic actress. She looks like she has been dropped from a height, and her expression and posture are full of life. Yet little milk has splashed onto her arms and legs and there is not a ripple on the surface. So the image is obviously styled (posed). The contrast between the natural and the posed makes us question what is real and what is constructed, which reflects our relationship to celebrity. When seeing pictures of famous people, we are never quite sure what is a true glimpse into their personality and what is a constructed image to make them look more glamorous or interesting. Leibovitz treads the border between the outer mask and the inner person. She rejects the idea that there is one truthful, objective way of representing a person.

> *I no longer believe there is such a thing as objectivity. Everyone has a point of view. Some people call it style, but what we're really talking about is the guts of a photograph. When you trust your point of view, that's when you start taking pictures.* ANNIE LEIBOVITZ

Creating colour

The picture is taken on a **medium format camera** with 6 x 6 cm square **colour transparency film**. This larger film gives the photograph great quality and detail. Leibovitz was one of the first people to mix natural and artificial light together, creating the effect of highly saturated (deep, rich) colour. Use of the bright studio flashlight meant she was able to use **slow film** to capture detail. This achieves the crisp, glossy effect usually required for magazine spreads and covers.

DUANE MICHALS

Duane Michals was born in the USA in 1932 and trained as a **graphic** designer in New York in 1956. It was a trip to the Soviet Union in 1958 that inspired him to start taking photographs seriously. His work is extremely personal and direct, dealing with themes such as love, fear, death and **identity**. He has exhibited worldwide and has had many books published.

Breaking rules

Michals' approach, techniques and subject matter are highly original, breaking the accepted rules of photography. He feels that a single photographic image is not adequate to communicate his interest in the changing nature of relationships, loss, memory and the imagination. To overcome the limitations Michals handwrites captions, poems and thoughts – sometimes whole pages – to go with his photographs. He is well known for using sequences of several photographs to tell stories and show the passing of time. Michals' commercial work is strikingly similar to his personal work. For his film **stills**, magazine and advertising photography, he works with minimum equipment and the available light. He likes to keep things simple and has no darkroom or assistants.

Making up stories

Although Michals' black and white images have a very natural feel, they are actually set up. **Documentary** photography can be faked and fool us into believing something is real when it is not. Michals, on the other hand, is very clear that his photographs are constructed (made up) stories used to express his ideas. He treats real streets and domestic locations like stage sets in which he can set up dramatic action with models. He creates a fictional world to deal with issues that concern him.

> *There's no other art form which reproduces reality with [photography's] kind of fidelity. But to me that is to say that appearances are the only things which we consider to be real. What about dreams, what about fear...? These experiences to me constitute [are] reality... The things that interested me were all invisible... things you never see on the street.* DUANE MICHALS

A Letter From My Father

In *A letter From My Father* (1975), Michals uses a real photo of his parents and his brother to reveal his own relationship with his father. Michals uses daylight, which gives the photograph a natural feel. The image is taken on a **35 mm camera**. He has focused on the father whose direct gaze makes the photograph feel honest. The younger man is slightly out of focus, but clear enough for us to see. We can guess this is a family but, with the mother figure half hidden, the main subject is the father-son relationship. Without the text the message of the image would be open to many interpretations. It would also be less emotional and intimate. The fact that the text is handwritten adds to the personal emotion of the image – it feels like reading someone's diary.

> *A photograph of my father doesn't tell me for a second what I thought about my father ... not that writing describes what you're looking at, but talks about what you can't see.* DUANE MICHALS

Tools and techniques

Michals uses various techniques to help him record and communicate the things we cannot see. His images often have a dreamlike feel. He uses multiple images, laying several shots on top of each other. Sometimes he uses **overexposure** so that parts of the image are given more light than others, appearing very bright. This visual effect of pure light is often used to communicate the sense of a person's spirit. In some pictures, the **shutter speed** is open for long enough to record movement in the scene as a blur.

The Illuminated Man *(1968). This is an example of overexposure used to make part of an image brighter than others.*

Poetry, paint and ideas

Michals has been called an amateur because he uses poetry and paint in a child-like, sometimes clumsy way. Michals, however, is not interested in technical perfection, only in communicating ideas. The unpolished, child-like look of his images adds to the effect of Michals' directness and vulnerability. The scrawled writing and the simple use of paint make our connection to the artist and his work more immediate and emotional. Michals has painted over famous photographs by renowned masters of photography, Ansel Adams (1902–84) and André Kértesz (1894–1985), which challenges what we accept as good photography.

Themes and influences

Michals' themes of death, love and loss are the kind of subjects often associated with writers, filmmakers and painters. Like the writer Lewis Carroll's *Alice...* stories and the **Surrealist** painters, Michals plays around with scale. He makes objects huge or tiny in the picture, leading us into the world of dreams and the unconscious.

Michals work links back to an earlier playfulness and experimentation with illusion seen in 19th century photographs. For example, Henry Peach Robinson (1830–1901), who used numerous shots to creates complex scenes, or the pictures of Julia Margaret Cameron (1815–79) where she dressed her sitters up as fairies and mythical figures.

The personal

Michals' photography often expresses how he feels about something. This self-revealing approach, along with the use of text, paved the way for many of today's artists such as Tracey Emin (b. 1963), whose artwork is confessional, incorporating diary-text and personal photographs. Michals is not frightened to talk about himself or be mocked. He does not hide what he thinks or feels, and risks embarrassment by his emotion and openness. Through his example, he urges us to have the courage to be individual and to take risks, despite the fear of ridicule. His images of loss, loneliness and ageing remind and urge us to seize pleasure in the present.

In this photograph, Madrid *(1958), Michals uses a slow shutter speed to show movement as a blur.*

MARTIN PARR

Martin Parr was one of the first serious **documentary** photographers to work in colour. Born in Epsom, in the UK, in 1952, he studied photography at Manchester Polytechnic from 1970 to 1973. Along with photographers such as Chris Killip (b. 1946) and Paul Graham (b. 1956), Parr was part of the revival of documentary photography in the 1970s. He has exhibited all over the world and had many books published. In 1994 Parr became a member of Magnum, the world's most influential photographic agency. He went on, in the 1990s, to also work on commercial projects – such as advertising assignments and television documentaries.

Observing everyday life

Parr is fascinated by ordinary life, which he reveals in his photographs as bizarre. He photographs a vast array of everyday subjects, from shopping trips and Tupperware parties to holidays and barbecues. He reflects our rituals, habits, hopes and pretensions back to us in a comic and often uncomfortable way.

Public aims

Parr makes serious social points through his work. He has recorded massive social change in the UK since the election of Margaret Thatcher as Prime Minister in 1979. Parr has observed how society has become much more consumer centred, instead of community centred. He has looked at how the idea of **class** has more to do with money now, instead of background and birth: how the old-fashioned, post-war idea of being looked after by the state and each other has been replaced by a more individualist culture where people are encouraged to look out for themselves. Parr was one of the first photographers to record his own social background – the suburban middle classes.

Stimulating debate

Parr's photographs have stimulated a debate about what it is **ethical** to photograph. Parr has been criticized for photographing people in an unsympathetic way and exposing their vanities and greed. Parr says his intention is to make serious comment about society, not to take portraits. He doesn't use people to present them as individuals – instead he chooses images that best show his views about society.

> *[I look] for the vulnerabilities you can get within a social situation. Unless it hurts, unless there's some vulnerability there, I don't think you're going to get a good photograph.* MARTIN PARR

Image 14 from The Last Resort, 1983–86

Parr took this photograph in New Brighton, as part of a series on this rundown, working-class seaside resort in the industrial northwest of England. The series was called *The Last Resort*. Parr took photographs in colour, using daylight mixed with on-camera flash (see box page 34). The effect removes any atmospheric or romantic mood. The flat, glaring flash-light gives his subjects a hard edge, seeming to expose them. There are no shadows to soften the effect of the baby's crying. The flash makes the colour vivid to the point of harshness: the parasol garishly reflects the red of the baby's howling face.

When Parr showed his images of New Brighton, the response was critical. Many people only saw litter and fast food. The rawness of the photographs offended some people who still had a romantic view of working-class people.

What these people missed was Parr's viewpoint as a new parent himself. He was genuinely interested in the way people coped with their children. We may see the woman in the photograph as uncaring, not listening to her child's cries. Or we can see her as arousing Parr's sympathy: she is coping on her own; she is tired but her eyes are open to her child's distress; the child is dressed nicely and sitting in a colourful, shady buggy. Perhaps it is not Parr who is snobbish, but the viewers who criticized him.

Using colour

Parr's use of colour in documentary photography helped it to be accepted as a serious **medium**. Previously colour pictures were largely associated with snapshots or used for commercial fashion and advertising photography. Colour was not considered serious enough for the gritty realism and social concerns of documentary photography.

Parr's use of colour becomes increasingly vivid as his work becomes more critical. His photographs' colourful shapes and forms are not beautiful, but brash – images of Union Jacks, fish and chips and bottles of beer are raw in their primary-coloured brightness. For his project *Common Sense* (1995–99), Parr photocopied his photographs of cigarette ends, sunburnt skin and fast food to exaggerate their harsh colour: the cheap reproduction and violent colour becomes part of Parr's criticism of global consumption and waste.

Fill-in flash

Fill-in flash is when flash-light is used with existing **ambient light**. For example, on a very sunny day, the subject might actually be in shadow, so it is useful to brighten up (fill-in) this shadow with flash. Flash-on-camera can be a harsh light, destroying all the mood of the existing play of light and shadow, so it should be used carefully. Some photographers, like Parr, use fill-in flash because of its harsh qualities. Parr says of photographs he took of superstores, 'the flash can help express the alienation which is so often the trademark of these large anonymous stores. It also ensures that all the detail in the face comes out'.

This untitled photo of a plate of food from Parr's Common Sense *project (1995–99) emphasizes harsh colour and waste.*

Popular culture and new methods

Parr loves popular culture and collects the kind of things a lot of people think of as kitsch: miners' plates, postcards and contemporary folk art. His work draws on high-street photography, postcards and seaside souvenirs.

Parr has made room installations where you walk into what feels like real rooms within an exhibition space. He has displayed his images as bright photocopies, collected 'boring postcards' for a book in 1999, and brought together photographs of himself taken in 'cheesy' portrait studios for *Autoportrait* (2000). The **still** images from Parr's television series *Sign of the Times* (1992), which documented popular taste, were displayed on bus stops, underground billboards and posters.

SEBASTIÃO SALGADO

Sebastião Salgado is renowned for photographing the world's poor. Born in Brazil in 1944, he trained as an economist (an expert who deals with the making, moving and use of money and wealth) and began working as a **photojournalist** in 1973. Salgado works on long projects that are published in magazines and books. He follows a tradition of **documentary** photography, working in black and white on a **35 mm camera** to witness and record the world. Salgado has exhibited worldwide and received numerous awards.

Images of injustice

Salgado considers himself a reporter, not an artist. He takes his photographs primarily in the developing (third) world – Africa, South America and parts of Asia – and his subjects range from starving refugees to destitute children. He is fascinated by the use, destruction and ownership of land. Salgado's aim is to highlight injustice and inequality in 'a world divided by excess and need'. He always captures his subject's dignity, which is echoed by the beauty of his images. It can feel uncomfortable to view his gorgeous pictures of poverty in a gallery, to get visual pleasure from looking at distress, starvation and hardship.

> *It's not my intent to give people a guilty conscience, just to make them think.* SEBASTIÃO SALGADO

Workers: Archaeology of the Industrial Age

Salgado photographed all over the world for a massive project called *Workers: Archaeology of the Industrial Age* (1993). He exhibited the work and collected 350 of the photographs into a book. The images document the endurance and skills of manual workers worldwide, before they are replaced by the increasing use of machines and computer technology. The book is called 'archaeology' because the traditional skills shown in the pictures progress from those used in the Stone Age and the **Industrial Revolution** through to the present day.

An important part of Salgado's work is his attempts to inform people. *Worker's ...* has a lengthy introduction and informative photo-captions to provide the reader with a social and historical background to the images. Much of the book shows how the developed Western world, such as the USA and western Europe, exploit developing countries. Salgado shows small traders being pushed out by international corporations, or Western companies profiting from low wages and poor conditions. Yet the book is also full of hope and celebration, recording the workers' positive spirit.

Travelling the world

> *I am from the Third World; I belong to that side of the fence. I am not angry, but I am emotional, we have a lot of work still to do.*
> SEBASTIÃO SALGADO

Salgado is passionate and tireless, constantly roving the world to document massive social, political and economic change. He researches each project thoroughly, planning his route and working with organizations that can help him contact the people he wants to photograph. His projects tend to be on a huge scale. With *Migrations* (1993–99) for example, Salgado spent 7 years documenting the displacement of millions of people across more than 35 countries. His photographs capture the torment of people who have no choice but to leave their country, often due to wars or because of economic hardship.

This photo from the Migrations *(1993–99) project is entitled* A Tower Air charter flight from Moscow to New York with 500 Passengers on board, 1994*.*

Serra Pelada Goldmine, Pará, Brazil, 1986

Serra Pelada Goldmine, Pará, Brazil, 1986 is one of the photographs from the project *Workers: Archaeology of the industrial Age*. It shows hundreds of men digging for gold in Brazil. Fifty thousand men were employed for this enormous task. Salgado has compared this grand manual project to the building of the pyramids in ancient Egypt by thousands of slaves. Salgado's photograph shows that the gold mine is broken into square plots. The mud-covered gold diggers appear tiny in the distance. The repetition of the shapes of the men and the plots creates a strong pattern. The **composition**, which reduces the men to ant-like sizes, suggests that they are not treated as individuals, but are employed in vast numbers for their physical ability to do the task. The figure in the foreground (centre) stands in contrast to the other anonymous workers. We see his face, clothes and body. He looks weary yet self-assured (confident). It reminds us that all the workers are individuals, but are not treated as such.

The pose of the foreground figure against the post reminds us of Christ on the Cross. Immediately associations and questions come to mind. Is this man a martyr in some way who suffers for other people, as Christ did? Is he a victim of the more powerful state? Salgado's work has been compared to medieval religious frescoes (wall paintings) which often show images of Christ in locations on a grand scale.

Black, white and in between

Salgado uses a wide-angle lens which makes the background figures look even more distant than they would to the eye. It exaggerates the mens' smallness and sameness. The image is composed largely of **mid-tones**. There are some pure blacks and whites but mostly the photograph is made up of all the grey tones in between. There is no great contrast or dramatic lighting, few bright **highlights** or deep shadows. Salgado achieved a surprising beauty by using perfect **exposures** in which exactly the right amount of light is let in through the lens on to the film. This subtle arrangement of grey tones throughout the image, and the repetition of shapes, cause the workers to look like a beautiful patterned background.

Colour makes me uneasy: black and white allows for more imagination, and I dream that way. I see the world in monochrome [without colour]. It is compassion and dignity, not colour, that allow you to see the world anew. SEBASTIÃO SALGADO

Can photography change anything?

Since the early 19th century, when Lewis Hine (1874–1940) took photographs of child labour in the USA, photographers have sought to expose social inequality. Powerful images taken by photographers such as Dorothea Lange (1895–1965) and Walker Evans (1903–1975) of American famine and migration in the 1930s created public outcry and the demand for government financial assistance. Don McCullin (b. 1935) and Larry Burrows (1926–1971) photographed the Vietnam War in the 1960s. When the American public saw these horrific images they withdrew their popular support of the war and many people believe that this contributed to America's defeat. Salgado's work in highlighting injustice is in the same tradition.

CINDY SHERMAN

Cindy Sherman is an influential art photographer who changed the way we look at photography. She was born in New Jersey, USA, in 1954 and graduated with a Photography degree from the State University of New York in Buffalo in 1976, where she initially studied Painting. She is now based in New York. Sherman's many photographic projects challenge the clichés and **stereotypes** found in the images and myths of popular culture. Her work helped move photography out of the photography galleries and into mainstream art galleries.

Views of women

In the 1970s, academics and feminists were already looking at the way images were used to convey messages in photographs, film and television. For example, the repetition of an image such as 'the dumb blonde' or 'the good mother' takes away any sense of a person's individuality and represents them as a stereotype. Feminists argued (and still do) for equal pay and equal opportunities for women in the workplace. They fought for women to be taken seriously as individuals and not just to be treated as sex objects or boring housewives. So the way women were represented in photographs played an important part in shifting people's attitude to, and expectations of, women. Sherman contributed to this debate. Through photography, Sherman encourages us to question its role in presenting a simplified, unrealistic and unfair view of women.

As in many of her photos, in Untitled Film Still 18 *Cindy Sherman has used herself as the model.*

Using herself as a model

Sherman uses herself as a model in many of her photographs. She is not trying to make autobiographical work. Instead she is imitating the different kinds of female roles found in films, newspapers, magazines and television. Sherman poses as a film heroine, pin-up girl and horror-movie victim. She is not aiming to record reality as she actually sees it, but to reveal how stories can be created by photography. By photographing herself in so many roles or 'guises', Sherman is showing us that the images cannot be photographs of the 'real' her. Instead they show us all the different people she can become by careful posing, dressing, **composition** and lighting.

Photography's hidden meanings

All photographs use visual and technical devices, such as lighting and framing, to create a mood or emphasize an idea. Sherman makes us aware of the devices that are used in photography, encouraging us to question images and reflect upon their meaning. Who took the photograph? Why? What does the photograph say about us and the culture we live in? By asking these questions we are able to understand the hidden meanings of images.

Horror and the bizarre

For photographic series in the 1980s, such as the *Untitled* and *Centrefolds*, Sherman produced huge colour prints. She gave them a commercial, glossy look so that her photographs bring to mind advertising shots and magazine spreads. Sherman's images become increasingly frightening and bizarre in her *Horror* series. She uses dolls, masks and artificial body parts for her models and the use of artificial lighting is exaggerated.

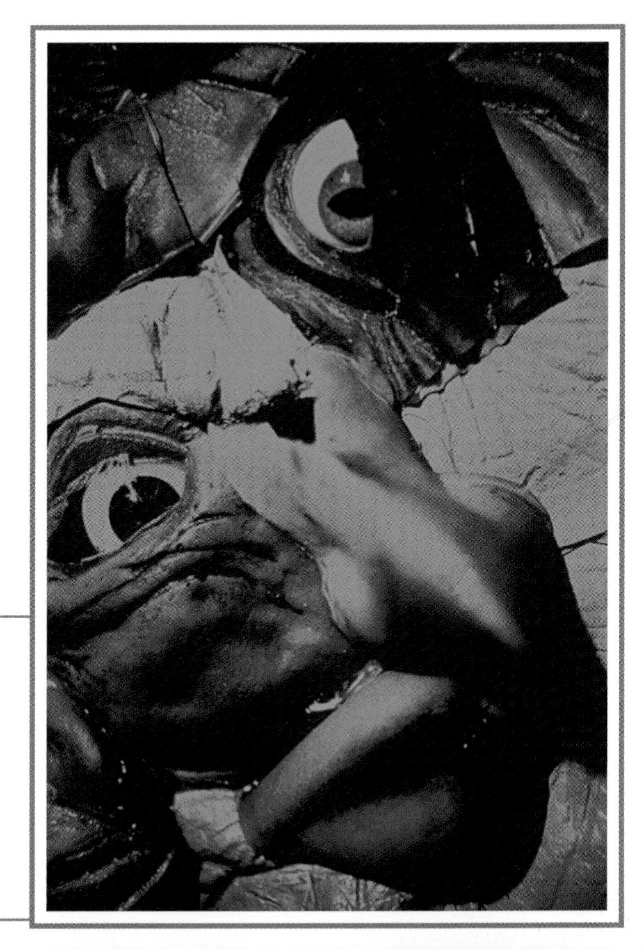

This is a close up of a mask in Untitled 314C *(1994) from the* Horror *series. Sherman presents us with our own fears by indicating the way they are shown on television or in films.*

Influences

Sherman draws on a whole range of popular imagery found, for example, in Hollywood glamour, fairy stories, historical portraits and television. Her work can be traced back through Andy Warhol (1928–87) and Claude Cahun (1894–1954) to Marcel Duchamp (1887–1968). Like them, she challenges the boundaries between art and the everyday by re-presenting familiar images or objects in a new context. Like the **Surrealists**, Sherman tapped into the part our imagination plays in both interpreting a picture and understanding the world that we live in.

Untitled Film Still 4

Sherman produced a series of around 70 small black and white photographs for *Untitled Film Stills* between 1977 and 1980. The pictures imitate images of women found in 1950s and 1960s 'B movies' (cheap budget popular films). Using herself as the model, Sherman poses as different traditional female stereotypes, such as the *femme fatale* (a glamorous woman who uses men to get what she wants), the victim and the dreaming housewife. She expresses their various hopes, and their boredom and anxieties.

> *When I prepare each character [for my photographs] ...I'm trying to make other people recognize something of themselves rather than me.* CINDY SHERMAN

In *Still 4* the figure of the female heroine leaning against a door in a shady corridor is a familiar type of film heroine. The woman's appearance – smart suit, fur jacket and neat bobbed hair – suggests a conventional 'good girl'. The corridor leads out of the scene, with dark shadowy lighting giving a sense of isolation and threat. The image has a feeling of danger off-scene – is the woman resting, knocking or listening at the door? Is she looking for help? We are encouraged to engage our imagination and create our own story.

At the same time as we are inventing a story, we know it is Sherman pretending to be the heroine. We know that the photograph is posed and that Sherman, as the photographer, is trying to make us respond in a certain way. This prompts two feelings: we can identify with and feel the vulnerability of the woman in the picture and at the same time we know that this is a fiction and not real. We are left with a sense of uncertainty – about the reality or truth of the photograph and about what we think and feel. Film visuals, advertising and magazine images work to make us believe the story in a picture, but Sherman invites us to understand the parts the picture-maker and our own imagination play in the construction of a photograph.

Techniques

In the *Film Stills* series, Sherman used natural lighting, black and white film and a **35 mm camera**. She set up the shots by carefully choosing a particular location and modelling and posing herself. To photograph herself for these shots, Sherman took the indoor pictures using a delayed-shutter release, and got friends and family to press the shutter for the outdoor shots.

JEFF WALL

Jeff Wall was born in Canada in 1946. He started as a painter and studied Fine Art and Art History at the University of British Columbia from 1964 to 1970. He took up photography in the 1970s and produces huge colour photographs, up to 5 metres across.

Wall displays his photographs in aluminium-framed boxes, lit up from behind like backlit advertising displays. The photographic scenes are in modern-day settings and make us think about life today. They show dramatic human action set in landscapes and interiors. Wall wanted photography to be taken seriously as part of the mainstream art world. He is considered to be a leading contemporary artist, and can be seen as a **Postmodernist** painter, using photography instead of oil and canvas. He has exhibited all over the world.

Construction and lighting

Wall plays around with photographing his scenes at different distances from the viewer. If the people appear far enough away they lose their individuality and become types of people doing typical things. In close-up, the people have a theatrical quality, which also stops us connecting with them personally. The gestures made by the people in his photographs are familiar and we recognize them as a type of human behaviour instead of a particular person's response. The titles emphasize, not the individuals, but the roles they play, for example in *Woman and her Doctor* (1980–81), or *The Guitarist* (1987).

Wall constructs his scenes carefully. The poses of the people and the lighting tend to look artificial. Wall's earlier images captured a dramatic moment that was really happening within a landscape. Later he used actors and computer technology to set up the scenes. The drama is often everyday and ordinary – for example, a man looking at an industrial landscape, or people meeting on the street. However, the poses of the people in the scenes, and the presentation of the pictures within huge illuminated frames, gives the pictures a highly dramatic feel. This mix of a real-life scene, presented in a theatrical way, gives us the sense of the overlap between real and acted life. Wall makes us think about the fact that people play roles, a bit like actors, in order to fit in with society.

The illuminated box

The size and rich colour of Wall's lightboxes remind the viewer of the sheen of an oil painting, a cinema screen or backlit street advertising. The lightboxes hang on the walls of galleries and their frames and brightness make the experience feel like looking through a window.

Influences and sources

Wall became interested in the art movement, Dada (see box), while studying Painting at college. He draws on themes from advertising, film and **documentary** photography and works like a film director with a team of people setting up and acting out the story in his photographs. Wall's dramatic moments, such as men shaking hands, street fights or a couple arguing, are like key scenes from films. The size and **composition** of Wall's pictures remind us of a variety of paintings and styles of images. He makes us compare different styles of picture-making as well as different periods of time. Wall is also inspired by Baroque art (see box). John Heartfield's disjointed **photomontages** of the 1920s, which challenged the realistic forms of photography and aimed to reveal the artificial nature of society, were an inspiration for Wall's complex computer-manipulated images.

Dada and Baroque

Dada: The term 'Dada' was coined in 1916 in Switzerland by a group of mainly painters and poets, to describe a new art movement. Dada questions what can be classified as art. It spread rapidly after the war throughout Europe and to the USA as both a reaction to the horrors of World War I and a challenge to traditional values. Dada did not have a particular style, but was provocative and interested in the role of chance in artistic creation. Dada paved the way for the **Surrealist** movement which began in 1924. Some famous Dada artists include André Breton (1896–1966) and Jean Arp (1888–1966).

Baroque: This was a movement of European art and architecture which began in Rome and dominated the art world in Europe from around 1600–1750. Baroque began as a reaction against the very formal and restrained style of Classicism and was characterized by ornate decoration and elaborate spatial effects. It combined the use of architecture, painting, sculpture, decoration and light and the end result was often theatrical and dramatic. Baroque art often features vivid scenes of miracles and the crucifixion. Sir Christopher Wren, architect of St Paul's Cathedral in London, was influenced by the Baroque movement, and some famous Baroque artists include Peter Paul Rubens (1577–1640) and Gian Lorenzo Bernini (1598–1680).

A Sudden Gust of Wind (after Hokusai)

Wall spent five months in 1993 researching and making *A Sudden Gust of Wind.* He photographed the various people, the sheets of paper and the landscape separately. From these many pictures he used computer technology to place the figures and the sheets of paper on to the landscape to make one image.

Like all Wall's photographs, *A Sudden Gust ...* , is displayed as a huge **colour transparency** which is fixed in an aluminium display case, backlit by fluorescent lights. The size (2.3 x 3.8 metres) is similar to that of a traditional oil painting. It is large enough to be viewed comfortably in spacious galleries.

With this photography Wall is recreating the tiny 19th century Japanese woodcut *Travellers caught in a sudden breeze at Ejiri*, from '*Thirty-six Views of the Fuji*', (c. 1832) by Katsushika Hokusai (see page 47). Through this recreation Wall makes a comparison between a modern and a traditional way of living, and between the different ways life can be represented in pictures. Wall often makes references to other images which gives his work several layers of meaning.

The action of Hokusai's figures appears against a calm rural landscape. Wall's figures are set against fields and water, but it is clearly a modern landscape with technology, pollution and human settlement visible. Wall has straightened the lines of the original Hokusai print by removing the curving path and the mountain. *A Sudden Gust* ... has a bleaker feel than the more romantic original. Instead of Mount Fuji, Wall's scene has telegraph poles towering above the horizon.

The flowing gowns of Hokusai's barefoot figures have been transformed into various uniforms of male Western work-wear: the office suit and the workman's hard hat and wellingtons. We are left to wonder about the men's relationships to each other. What work roles are these men playing? Are the suited men the bosses? The men all react in the same way to a sudden gust of wind and, for a moment, they are freed from playing the roles their jobs impose on them. The men's spontaneous movement looks comic and ridiculous – there is a flowing scarf where a man's head should be. A moment of joyous chaos lets the men break out of the social framework. What society expects of the men and what they expect of themselves is temporarily lifted. They are no longer professional people of varying status, but are all bent double and helpless in response to nature.

> *In the drama, [there is] ... a moment in which the personalities undergo an experience which places their existence in question.*
> JEFF WALL

GILLIAN WEARING

Gillian Wearing uses photography and video to explore everyday life and human behaviour. Born in 1963 in Birmingham, UK, Wearing graduated with a Fine Art degree at Goldsmith College, London, in 1990. She won the Turner Prize in 1997 and is part of the 1990s 'Young British Art' movement. Although Wearing engages with real people in the real world, her work rejects traditional **documentary** photography. She does not want to photograph people in order to literally show real life. Instead, she wants to portray modern life by interacting with the people in her work. She acknowledges that the presence of a camera can change people's behaviour. Wearing's art can be confessional, funny, disturbing and moving.

> *For me, one of the biggest problems with pure documentary photography is how the photographer ... engineers something to look like a certain kind of social statement – for instance, you can make someone look miserable, when this is just one side ... I couldn't bear the idea of taking photographs of people without their knowing.* GILLIAN WEARING

Working with the people

Wearing lets the people she is filming know she is taking pictures. She gives them a voice by getting them to write text, speak or react to something she has set up. Wearing sometimes recreates what she has seen to avoid exposing or embarrassing the real people. With her video *Dancing in Peckham* (1994), Wearing videos herself dancing in the street to an imaginary soundtrack, instead of filming the real woman she saw. Wearing's interest in people is central to her work. She is fascinated by how people express their individuality and behave socially. *Dancing in Peckham* questions why it is acceptable to dance on your own. Wearing looks at how we are controlled by authority, social expectations and our own inhibitions.

Techniques

Wearing works with video, photography, text and sound. She uses ordinary snapshot prints from **colour negative film** that are **processed** at the local chemists. She is not interested in high-quality art prints, but in producing something that connects to real people. Wearing says 'I can't bear the idea of technology being something that represents me. The thing that goes through my head is not the technology, but what I want to do, with whom, and when and what inspires me.'

Influences

Wearing draws on the 1970s 'fly-on-the-wall' TV documentaries of real people in which the subjects reveal themselves to camera. But, as in Wearing's work, they do so knowingly, with consent and some control.

Help

For Wearing's project *Signs that say what you want them to say not signs that say what someone else wants you to say* (1992–93) she approached strangers on the street. She asked them to write down what they were thinking, then photographed them with their sign. Often the person writes something surprising. In *Help*, the policeman's sign is a good example because what we expect from a policeman is to give us help and not to receive it from us. The photographs challenge the judgements we make about people based on their appearance, which is what we usually do when looking at photographs. With only the image for information, it is like our first impressions of someone before they speak. We make judgements about people that are often wrong and always simplistic. So with the *Signs...* project Wearing challenges the reality of more traditional photography.

TIMELINE

1827	Niecephore Niepce and Daguerre make a daguerreotype – a light sensitive image on metal
1839	William Henry Fox Talbot discovers how to make the first photograph
1904	First colour photographs, autochromes, marketed by the Lumiére brothers
1908	Henri Cartier-Bresson is born
1932	Duane Michals is born
1939	William Eggleston is born David Hockney is born
1944	Sebastião Salgado is born
1945	World War II ends
1946	Jeff Wall is born
1947	Magnum photographic agency is founded
1949	Annie Leibovitz is born
1952	Martin Parr is born
1954	Cindy Sherman is born
1955	Andreas Gursky is born The Family of Man exhibition, Museum of Modern Art, New York
1958	Nick Knight is born
1959	Joy Gregory is born
1963	Gillian Wearing is born
1976	Eggleston's solo exhibition Colour Photographs at The Museum of Modern Art, New York, USA
1977	Wall makes his first lightbox
1977–80	Sherman makes her *Untitled Film Stills* series
1979	Margaret Thatcher elected as Conservative Prime Minister in Britain
1982	Hockney begins 4–5 years of experimenting with the camera
1983	Leibovitz becomes *Vanity Fair's* first contributing photographer, has her first solo exhibition and publishes her first book

1984	Duane Michals' touring solo exhibition in the UK
1985	American Images exhibition, Barbican Art Gallery, London UK is criticized for not having a wide appeal and for being unpolitical
1986	Martin Parr's *The Last Resort* is shown at the Serpentine Gallery, London, UK Nick Knight starts working with Yohji Yamamoto
1989	The Berlin wall comes down. **Communist** regimes end in Hungary, Poland, East Germany, Czechoslovakia, Bulgaria and Romania Through the Looking Glass exhibition, Britain's last great exhibition of Photographic Art takes place Nelson Mandela released from prison in South Africa End of apartheid in South Africa
1997	Gillian Wearing's work is exhibited in the Sensation exhibition, Royal Academy of Arts, London, UK – a significant and controversial show representing Young British Artists Gillian Wearing wins the Turner Prize
1998	Andreas Gursky wins the Citibank prize. His work is exhibited at The Photographers' Gallery, London, UK
2001	Joy Gregory's Traces exhibition, London, UK, including the image *Elegance*
2002	Sebastião Salgado exhibits *Exodus* at the Barbican Gallery, London, UK
2003	Cindy Sherman exhibition at the Serpentine Gallery, London, UK

GLOSSARY

35 mm camera small format camera taking 35 mm film with 35 mm x 24 mm negatives
abstract art that does not represent figures or objects
ambient light existing light which could be daylight and/or indoor light
candid photographing people when they are unaware, thus catching a natural photograph of what is happening
class system which divides society up into sections depending on how much money they have or what background they come from, for example, upper class, middle class and lower class
colour negative (film) kind of colour film used for snapshots. After the pictures are taken, the film is made into a strip of images where the colours and tones are opposite to how they really were – called negatives. From these negatives, positive photographic prints are made.
colour transparency (film) after the pictures are taken, the film is made into a strip of images where the colours and tones appear as they did in real life. The film can be cut up and mounted into slides for projection on a screen.
Communism/Communist economic system that seeks to distribute wealth evenly in a situation of economic plenty
composition how the different elements of an image are arranged
crop to print only part of the image taken on the film
documentary aiming at presentation of reality
electron microscope microscope that makes use of a beam of electrons instead of light
ethical consider the moral rights and wrongs about doing something
exposure light from the scene in front of the camera goes through the lens and falls on the film when the shutter on a camera is pressed. The film is then exposed to light in order to make a picture of the scene.
Expressionist art movement in which artists show a distorted image of reality in order to express their own emotions
fix chemicals used, or the process of using chemicals, to keep the photographic image on film or paper so that it does not go darker on exposure to more light
fixed lens lens with set focal length, for example standard lens, telephoto lens, wide-angle lens (not a zoom lens which can change focal lengths)
format refers to size and shape of the camera film
graphic clear and vivid imagery
graphics imagery – painting, print, illustration or diagram – usually used on a printed page
highlights brightest areas of a photograph
identity characteristics that determine who or what a person is
Industrial Revolution time of invention and new developments in industry where manual labour was replaced by machines. It began in Britain in the 18th century.

large format camera camera which uses one sheet of film. It can be a 5 x 7-inch (12.5 cm x 18 cm) or 10 x 8-inch (25.5 cm x 20 cm) camera, taking single sheets of film of that size.
medium channel, such as photography or sculpture, through which communication or expression takes place
medium format camera camera using film with 6 cm x 6 cm or 6 cm x 4 cm exposures
mid-tones all the greys (dark to light) between black and white in an image
motif object or symbol characteristic of a particular artist or movement
negative-positive reverse image on a film, with black tones showing as white and white tones showing as black. This converts into the correct tones when made into a paper print.
overexposure when film is given more light than it needs, appearing very bright
photochemistry chemicals used to make photographs
photo-collage one image made up of lots of images stuck next to each other
photograms images produced on photographic paper using photographic chemicals and light without the use of a camera
photojournalism taking photographs for use in magazines and newspapers
photomontage photograph made up of a selection of different photographs
Pop Art 1960s art movement that draws on popular images or culture
post-digital manipulation use of a computer to change a photograph after it is taken
Postmodern/Postmodernist art movement starting mid 1970s which uses art and popular imagery to question reality and representation and underlying motivation and ideas
processing making exposed film into negatives by a series of liquid chemical processes
reportage journalistic style, bringing an account of the news
shutter speed length of time that the film is exposed to light while the shutter is open
slow film film which is used in bright light, has fine detail and a good tonal range
standard lens lens which shows the scene with the same proportions, distance and perspective as the human eye. For a 35 mm camera, it is a 50mm lens.
stereotype person or thing that is considered to represent a conventional type
stills photographs taking still pictures from the moving scene of films
Surrealist art movement, begun in the 1920s, that was inspired by dreams and fantasies and the unconscious
telephoto lens long lens which brings distant subjects closer
tungsten light indoor household lights or photographic lights which make an orange colour-cast on photographs
typography use of type for printing
wide-angle lens short lens which covers a wide range, makes objects appear more distant

KEY WORKS

JOY GREGORY
The Beauty Project (1994) 'Autograph', Monograph
Memory & Skin (1998) 'Continental Drift – 10 Photographic Commissions'

ANDREAS GURSKY
Siemens, Karlsruhe (1991)
Rhine (1996)
Untitled V1 (1997)

DAVID HOCKNEY
Luncheon at the British Embassy Tokyo, *16 Feb 1983*
Pear Blossom Highway (1986)

ANNIE LEIBOVITZ
The Rolling Stones on the Road (1975)
John Lennon and Yoko Ono, NY city, December 8, 1980
Mikhail Baryshnikov & Linda Dowdell, White Oak plantation, Florida, 1990

NICK KNIGHT
100 most fashionable people, 1985 – i-D archives
Series of disabled models, *Dazed and Confused* Magazine, issue 46

DUANE MICHALS
Questions without Answers (1994)
A Letter From My Father (1975)

MARTIN PARR
The Last Resort, photographs of New Brighton, Merseyside (1986) Promenade Press
The Cost of Living (1989) Cornerhouse
Common Sense (1995–99)

SEBASTIÃO SALGADO
Workers: an archaeology (1993) N.Y. Aperture
Migrations (2000) Aperture
The Children (2000) Aperture

CINDY SHERMAN
Untitled Film Stills (1977–80)
Horror Pictures (1995)

JEFF WALL
The Destroyed Room (1978)
Restoration (1993)

GILLIAN WEARING
Signs *that say what you want them to say not what other people want them to say ...'* (1992–93)
*Confess All On Video. Don't Worry You Will Be in Disguise. Intrigued? Call Gillian (*1994) video

WHERE TO SEE WORKS

Here are galleries where the photographs mentioned in this book can be seen. Ring to find out what is currently on show before you go:

The Victoria and Albert Museum Archives, London, UK – The museum has a massive photography archive.

The Tate Modern and *Tate Britain, London, UK* – They have Andreas Gursky, David Hockney, Cindy Sherman, Martin Parr and Gillian Wearing in their collection.

The Photographers' Gallery, London, UK – This is a key venue for contemporary photography in Britain, with two buildings and several gallery spaces. It always has interesting contemporary photography on display.

The National Museum of Photography, Film and Television, Bradford, UK – This is a great place to learn more about the history of photography, advertising photography, documentary photography and digital technology.

Australian National Gallery of Art, Canberra, Australia – Displays collections of photographs.

National Museums of Merseyside, Walker Art Gallery, Liverpool, UK – Displays collections of photographs.

The following web sites show photographs by the photographers featured in this book:

www.iniva.org/xspaceprojects/gregory/ – Joy Gregory
www.martinparr.com
www.mastersofphotography.com
www.artchive.com

FURTHER READING

The History of Photography, Beaumont Newhall (Secker & Warburg, 1982)
Andreas Gursky Photographs (Schirmer Art Books, 1998)
Hockney on Photography – conversations with Paul Joyce (Cape, 1988)
Annie Leibovitz Photographs 1970–1990 (Harper Collins, 1991)
Nicknight, Nick Knight (Schirmer/Mosel, 1994)
Flora, Nick Knight and Sandy Knapp (Schirmer/Mosel, 1997)
The Essential Duane Michals, Marco Livingstone (Thames & Hudson, 1997)
Martin Parr, Val Williams (Phaidon, 2002)
Workers: an archaeology, Sebastião Salgado (N.Y. Aperture, 1993)
Cindy Sherman, Cindy Sherman (Thames & Hudson, 1997)
Jeff Wall, Kerry Brougher (L.A. Museum of Contemporary Art, 1997)
Gillian Wearing, R.Ferguson, D.De Salvo, J.Slyce (Phaidon, 1999)

INDEX